POETRY BOOKS BY STEPHEN BETT

Lift Off: a journey of future tense
Shall We Dance That One Around Again?
Back Principles: a book of spiritual fatigue
though we are incredibly small
Our Own Stunned Heads
Un/Wired
The Gross & Fine Geography: New & Selected Poems
Those Godawful Streets of Man: a book of raw wire in the city
Breathing Arizona: A Journal
Penny-Ante Poems: a book of break down
Sound Off: a book of jazz
Re-Positioning
Track This: a book of relationship
S PLIT
Extreme Positions
Sass 'n Pass
Three Women
Nota Bene Poems: A Journey
High-Maintenance
Trader Poets
High Design Refit
Cruise Control
Lucy Kent and other poems

MEMOIR BY STEPHEN BETT

So Got Schooled: in the tower, on the field (three memoirs)

BROKEN GLOSA:

an alphabet book of post-avant glosa

Stephen Bett

chax press 2023

ISBN 978-1-946104-42-7

Library of Congress Control Number: 2023937877

Chax Press
1517 N Wilmot Rd no. 264
Tucson Arizona 85712-4410

Chax Press books are supported in part by individual donors and by sales of books. Please visit *https://chax.org/membership-support/* if you would like to contribute to our mission to make an impact on the literature and culture of our time.

We thank our current assistant, Erica Cruz, for her work on Chax projects. Our Art Director, Cynthia Miller, contributes to all books Chax publishes.

FOREWORD

Stephen Bett's innovative *Broken Glosa* poems are neither simple nor predictable tributes to other poets; they are interactions, co-conspiracies, interrogations, and confessions to other poets—what it means to live in that element, that community which transcends time and place and is so dismissively referred to as "language." For there is a complex yet fluid interaction within these interconnected poems, between the poet and the subject writer glossed, the poet and his own text, the poet and language itself, an interaction that seems almost nodal in quality, a place where different dimensions coalesce. I am struck as well by how much intense work and creativity is woven into these glosas, by the way this poet's mind sparks with energy, the way this atemporal kind of writing seems utterly expressive of how the mind actually moves: a non-lineal, tenuous connectedness, the phenomenology (even) of the poem itself. And what strikes me most fundamentally is that I get more flashes of caught-in-the-interstices language-testing from any single one of Stephen Bett's glosa poems than from the entire collected works of other writers celebrated today. So this is a book of poems to be outright championed.

— *Ken Cathers*

The poems in Broken Glosa evolve, inform, and feed off one another. Their alphabetical ordering is so important—you can feel the tension of the process: the impacted with the flamboyant. These glosas potentiate the already minimal while, too, there's explosion, and the flying bits are fractals of the biographical heart. Big Bang stuff, a condensing and expanding in zero-time. Follow the dancing ball: the home it takes you to is not the one you left. There's emotion lurking for sure, as underscore, but the poems' pure elan and energy, their jazzy shortness of breath and pixie hijinks render the heavy lifting of such challenging work as feather-light. This is a really fascinating book—from tricky, resistant, clever to wise, giving, gratifying, and always sonically interesting and funny, funny! Stephen Bett's lifetime with poetry (reading it, writing it, teaching it) makes this book a kind of inverted Festschrift. These highly experimental glosa poems are strange, intricate little machines; I've never seen anything quite like them. And that's what I look for and appreciate most in art, something full of integrity and surprise. Bravo!

— *Michael Kenyon*

With immense gratitude

to Ken Cathers & Michael Kenyon

for their continued encouragement

throughout the writing of this book

Contents: the Poems

Rae Armantrout: I put a glose on you

Habitat-themed enclosure.
Zen-inflected mug.

Around the block
dogs bark at absence.

Habitat (entire poem) — Rae Armantrout *(with nods to Perloff, Silliman, & Alan Price)*

Habitat-themed enclosure.

I put a glose on you

(after the *cabeza*)

No to walleyed zone-outs

Zen-inflected mug.

Pitch-faced in its cups

or sinister vertigo effects

And no, I aint lyin' …

Around the block

headed for juiced circuits

attenuated hypotaxis

Always runnin' around …

dogs bark at absence.

The gap in the fence

koan-flaked inflection

How put a spell on you …

Charles Bernstein: the extension of Rrose Sélavy

War is the extension of prose by other means.
War is conflict resolution for the aesthetically challenged.
War is a casualty of truth just as truth is a casualty of war.
War is never having to say you're sorry.

War Stories — Charles Bernstein *(with a honk to CB's essays)*

War is the extension of prose by other means.

Raw is the pretension of Rrose Sélavy by other memes

Man Ray's sneeze on the found man's sleaze

Raw *may be a language poet and not know it…*

War is conflict resolution for the aesthetically challenged.

Raw is LangPo's solution to the alt-right falanged

Silly man *makes the social materiality of language more… opaque*

Raw *may be a language poet and not know* it's an airborne flake…

War is a casualty of truth just as truth is a casualty of war.

Raw lang is *not about deconstruction but about reconstruction* & more

Raw poe *is a mode of rhetoric, not an expansion of unmediated truth*

Raw *may be a lang poet & not know* that freak in bed called urban Ruth…

War is never having to say you're sorry.

Raw is *an aversion to the conservative dogmas* of worry

Raw *pragmatist poetics of language rejected a hermeneutics of suspicion*

Raw *may be a L=A=N=G=U=A=G=E poet & not know* its due commission…

Ted Berrigan:
The Do Nothing Congress of '48

It's 2 a.m. at Anne & Lewis's which is where it's at
On St. Mark's Place hash and Angel Hairs on our minds
Love is in our heart's (what else?) dope & Peter Schjeldahl*
Who is new and valid in a blinding snowstorm

80th Congress — Ted Berrigan *(with nods to his collaborator, Dick Gallup, & to Lita H.)*

It's 2 a.m. at Anne & Lewis's which is where it's at

except for Ron's, Dick's & Joe's (& Tom's now

I think of it, & Aram's too) some *funny horse play*

@ 2nd gen coterie for 15 of hop along & saddle up

On St. Mark's Place hash and Angel Hairs on our minds

On hi C, Le Metro & adventures in I do this

I do that Coke & coke a maverick cow-poke

w/ Alice & Anselm (1 & 2) groovin on yr take 'n toke

Love is in our heart's (what else) dope & Peter Schjeldahl

collating sonnet lines at 3 a.m., chromatic variations

Gysin cut-up & shufflin' off to Tulsaloo, lovely

Lita give us a wink & make me think of you

Who is new and valid in a blinding snowstorm

not to say relevant doing powder lines, no sexual congress

Grossman's Tavern Downchild Blues Band oh man

speeding at 4 a.m., & nothing for you with Truman

* sic

Paul Blackburn: Shall we dance?

Shall we dance that one around again?
  dance it beyond perfection?
  The celebrated and most knowing accents
putting the question.

Old — Paul Blackburn *(with a nod to Clayton Eshleman)*

Shall we dance that one around again?

twist again, like we did last summer …

brisk strokes w/ troubadour folks

but deft like your own Franz Kline

dance it beyond perfection?

mobile half-stanzas, tight a-

symmetrical turns

perfection is at best sketchy

The celebrated and most knowing accents

say it again / upper limit *musica*

tilt the pitch, brakes to all that

halting song (like you do

putting the question

full-throated gasp, or it

sat broken up under

your nose

George Bowering: Scatter-Gun

I went to the blackberries
on the vine.
They were blackberries
on the vine.

Against Description — George Bowering

I went to the blackberries

that old impulse, but didn't yak about it

his favourite colour yellow / May / number 27

his unlucky 52 & name-drop D. McF, sigh …

on the vine.

said gimme som'a dat light-footed black-

berry wine, it's beyond description [1]

so cover me in juice

[1] "Describers are tourists who leave milk cartons at the campsight [sic]." (G.B.)

They were blackberries

yah, don't tell, it's the "show me" state

here in the ol' Human Universe, straight

from his open mouth, no cracks (pls)

on the vine.

ouch, it's all so Thea-retical, yr daughter stomped

on my stocking feet scatter-gun & no we're not

doing Bök today, no OuLiPo left in our DNA

Ken Cathers: the sum

(for Ken)

are we no more
than skin
sewn over desire

unremembered flesh

the serial husband — Ken Cathers (*with the slightest nod to WCW*)

are we no more

than the sum of

the heart's frailest

missing pieces

than skin

if it comes to that

stretched cruel

& unusually thin

sewn over desire

which cuts a thousand ways

like lingchi's slow dice

dance across flesh

unremembered flesh

awake now to a descent

that lashes endless &

at odds with desire

Tom Clark: Outlier Onward

Early morning light archery
Moon pictures propped on the dawn gestalt
A plum violet flood of light
As I walked out into it once again

Walking Out — Tom Clark

Early morning light archery

ultimate soft target Great Naropa Poetry Wars

to Lang Po group-think-thunk thud

w/ allegories pissing up R. Maud (R. Mutt?)

this spaced out raw (worthy) ace shooter

Moon pictures propped on the dawn gestalt

came a long sunny acid salad days eating

pusi(ll)animous spirit in sky church (gulp)

high flying in & out of the garbage pail

A plum violet flood of light

early morning shenani'berrigans peaking

au naturel tripping the broad-beams

can't believe we're here again stone sober

As I walked out into it once again

full circle now wow peeking down on us all

primo uno gutsy feisty independista

outlier onward, & still un-co-opted!

Clark Coolidge: Maintenance

belonging to slow the means day in the period
of a tree a book as by the stretch to right
milk legitimate legs
or of a group long or on side

excerpt from The Maintains — Clark Coolidge

belonging to slow the means day in the period

or of a group long or on side

of a tree a book as by the stretch to right

milk legitimate legs

of a tree a book as by the stretch to right

milk legitimate legs

belonging to slow the means day in the period

or of a group long or on side

milk legitimate legs

or of a group long or on side

of a tree a book as by the stretch to right

belonging to slow the means day in the period

or of a group long or on side

belonging to slow the means day in the period

milk legitimate legs

of a tree a book as by the stretch to right

Robert Creeley: Company of Others

why not, buy a goddam big car,

drive, he sd, for
christ's sake, look
out where yr going.

I Know a Man — Robert Creeley *(with lil' nods to Dylan & the Creel himself)*

why not, buy a goddam big car,

question for the dummies & generic Johns:

was that a real poem or did you

just make it up yourself?

drive, he sd, for

yr own caution: hair-trigger turns, small

fist of words, elliptically, on impact

... see the light come shining ...

christ's sake, look

apropos that circumstance, that

possibility, momently, like they say

any day now, a•n•y day now …

out where yr going.

surrender, its own unfolding

drive, he said, we *know* this

blessèd company of others

Frank Davey: Google U

We have found 89 people in the UK with the name Frank Davey. Click here…
Frank Davey Bricklaying Pty Ltd. Report this listing as incorrect.
Frank Davey —Boxer… Global ID, 271827. sex, male. division, welterweight.
What is the nationality of Frank Davey, the Canadian writer?

View Frank Davey's Poetics — Frank Davey (*with further nod to Frank Davey, & to Google*)

We have found 89 people in the UK with the name Frank Davey. Click here…

All the Franks Davey, incl the Bardy Google guy, from Google U

"reinventing formal boundaries within the framework of our wired world"

Be the first to comment on payment promptness Frank Davey LTD…

Frank Davey Bricklaying Pty Ltd. Report this listing as incorrect.

Let's be frank… because frankly it's beyond about partytime:

Report laying a poem, how to lay one, lay dump & smack it to rest

Frank Davey & Co Funeral Directors in Hassocks, BN6. Contact them today…

Frank Davey — Boxer… Global ID, 271827. sex, male. division, welterweight.

Google yr own name, the one & only "Norfolk Police & Crime Commissioner

… aims to make Norfolk's future safe & secure, Vote Stephen, the safe bet."

Frank Davey, an unsuccessful gay, the first man he hit on (1924) married his sister.

What is the nationality of Frank Davey, the Canadian writer?

Er, um, A-murican'o colonial'o ? TISH imperialist lackey running dog

digital poeticker & mugger at Dog Shows, let me pen you an Open Letter:

Frank Davey writes nasty, vicious lies about me and my dog Boomer.

Ed Dorn: Slap'o Slap'o, Daddy-o

In soccer / when you do something good
you get a hug and a kiss

In american football / when you do [ditto]
you get a slap on the ass.

The Sociology of Games — Ed Dorn *(with a touching nod to Derrida)*

In soccer / when you do something good

something mo' comes back / in spades (& shades)

sump'ting saves the day, makes hay / on the ol' post-plantation

Paid yr money now git it on the ride, road-tester

you get a hug and a kiss

you get a Europass zone-out, zonk'o

you win your spurs up the yid army

you get a peck & you're faced ('n spaced)

In american football / when you do [ditto]

that ten percent amo a'muricano numero uno el afraid'o

factors upwards (pigskin-wise) ditto schmitto LGBT QPR'o [2]

while beyond the touchline there is nothing, queenie

you get a slap on the ass

that a'muricano macho aggro loverlie'o

homo-eroticismo beats thart thar's

homophobi'o, beats it big league

up, down, & off, slap'o slap'o, daddy-o

---

[2] Queens Park Rangers (not to be confused with Lady Di's Sloane Rangers

Craig Dworkin: The Déjà Vu of Déjà Dit

foreign part-
iculates stag
-nated on thy
tongue

Acquisition of Languish (entire pom) — Craig Dworkin

foreign part-

icles in the *déjà vu* of *déjà dit*

it's a post-LangPo Mo

— say again?

iculates stag

nights hunt motes in

the eye of the Dept

of Anguish

-nated on thy

conceptual poets 30 years

behind Hearsay Art

mind the gap!

tongue

-hold one appropriated

letter at a

time

William Everson (Brother Antoninus): a spiritual crisis

Nailed. Split. Crucified. Scourged.

* * *

I suffer the lance.
I faint on the sexual cross
Of this Mexican madness.

I Nail My Life — Brother Antoninus *(with nods to Donne & to dear David Meltzer)*

Nailed. Split. Crucified. Scourged.

Nailed, splitto'd, which dost thou more desire

pre-Easter or post, my-see-ya [3] or no

when no-see-ums bite

I suffer the lance.

Hanging on for the cavalry (a lot

the Mack 'n Funk brigade

the Heysus Sem troupe

[3] rimes with Nicea?

I faint on the sexual cross

This, no cheap party feint

(like we done before, in extremis)

Batter mine art, three-person'd King Con [4]

Of this Mexican madness.

Borg'd, Crossan'd & Spong'd

don't bug me who Rose [5]

—these guys are mine

---

[4]Constantine's Council *declares* trinity doctrine
[5]the Rose of Solitude

Patrick Friesen: Dear Harmon

miles davis cupping his trumpet with a mute,
a slippery sound, almost an escape, a caesura,
hold, *hold what? my breath, yes, but the watery*
applause in some club as well, bill evans having

mri — Patrick Friesen *(with nods to a better bet)*

miles davis cupping his trumpet with a mute,

dear harmon: that full round tone / &

sound bites /… can break / the heart

in / every / single / groove (doo bop bop

a slippery sound, almost an escape, a caesura,

a pause mid-zone or modal, like *so what* in the gut

nothing left … that / freakish, frenetic /

cartoonish / bop (we stack & cheat the poem

hold, *hold what? my breath, yes, but the watery*

choked 'n dented mute, hold yr breath in the mri, mr. b

yes, release molly b, & hold again for a count of ten

exquisite interjections / into blank space (spunk tube

applause in some club as well, bill evans having

flown the dupe, beel i'vaanz (en paree) weird & wired…

we had, by then / like totally / fused

(post-bop & cool blue u

Robert Grenier: Dazed at the Beach (a double-hinged saloon door glosa)

I can't talk and
look out the window
and talk at
the same time

imagine night if you
if you couldn't go
in the direction that you
that you know

Two glosa texts: *I can't* and *imagine night if you (full four-line poem)* — Robert Grenier *(with nods to ol' e.e., Led Zee, & Bobbie D, plus a wee dash of Spice)*

I can't talk and

listen to this work [6]

been dazed & confused

so long it's not true

look out the window

hear not just the sea

vibration hung a sand groove,

never bargained for you

[6] Fragmented four ways as each stanza's second line: *To listen to this work is to hear not just the sea at the end of the beach but the ocean in the midst of our words.* — Charles Bernstein [referring to Grenier's *A Day at the Beach*]

and talk at

the end of the beach

gone south, a clockwork wreck

things you should never do

the same time

ocean in our words

sand in mouth too

wet all over, that ol' teen glue [7]

imagine night if you

listen to this work

instead of stop to think you

begin to feel o baby i-o-u

if you couldn't go

hear not just the sea

voices all those years beachied

quick,[8] tangled up in blue

---

[7]Dave Clark Five
[8]Excuse bad poet-name pun

in the direction that you

at the end of the beach

stymie very stone barrier [9]

fence off more than a few

that you know

the ocean in our words,

we are a coastal people no-

thing but emptiness in our eyes

[9]Homage, collating Vera Frenkel, Very Stone Press, early days / daze

Anselm Hollo: The Crisis Spirituel Continues

on the high plains,
when we meet
the inspector
we say, "buenas tardes [inspector

High Plains Drifting (full poem) — Anselm Hollo *(for bob grenier, 13 september 81)*

on the high designer bar,

when we tip

the barista

we say, "no problema [barista

High Design Refit, After Hollo — yrs truly *(from* High-Maintenance*)*

on the high plains

es designer bar'do el frappo

when we go hi we don't

stay there for long

when we meet

& greet & tip the bean there pastor-

ship it can trip us up like

praise the lord / pass the loot

the inspector

que barista at the altarista

smack'd out un segundo

maladie du doute (oh

we say, "buenas tardes [inspectōr

no problema you're too late

we've already gone home on the

para nada of diddly squat

D. G. Jones: All Dis Palaver

his anguage fowts the aw of the father

•   •   •

the addy's sentence ooks
re-markaby ike daddy's dooded over
with some many spendourd pensis

Steve McCaffery on Pataphysics — D. G. Jones

his anguage fowts the aw of the father

dat gauge doubts an awl cld dent dis palaver

dose cadaver en famille wore mine anglophone h'art

due ouest dere gon' don' enclave @ N. Hatley

the addy's sentence ooks

like penitence from all dese spooks

ein vatch dat kaput da nacht [10]

mien solitude [11] binned in our mist

---

[10]Hugh MacLennan got too close to da family
[11]Twice too close

re-markaby ike daddy's dooded over

zee-ro marks for a gabby lover's udder

pupa's brand new jag physic'd in za drop zone

pour leaf clover dat wuz mama's only grown

with some many spendourd pensis

2B spent dicks wld sow no tricks

dis end of da line o bag a nickel or dime

ancien régime dere's nuttin left to mine

Michael Kenyon: Sticky Between Buttons

(for M)

Crappy corny tacky. Spinoza. Moody Blues. Stones. Yes. River. Pink Floyd. Yes. Pond. In a way. In a kind of round-about-imponderable-guessy touch-as-touch-can come-as-you-may don't-freak-the-kids way. Yes. That way.

Ghost — Michael Kenyon *(with nods to the jazzers & the rockers)*

Crappy corny tacky. Spinoza. Moody Blues. Stones. Yes. River. Pink

Mack 'n Cheesy (again). Spins yr Zola top. Cos you gotta… *Go* Now. Sticky

between buttons. Sam's on Yonge, 1971.[12] No? Stein way'd in at Herbie

& Joni's.[13] Bandied about Big Pink, & don't forget Ketil's *River* [14] darlin'

Floyd. Yes. Pond. In a way. In a kind of round-about-imponderable-

Yes'way. No'way. MK puts it away. We float a bond 'n wing it

peaking still. On the dark side. 'Round about midnight, shall be

ree-leas'd. Wigged out end of day touch-&-go roué

---

[12]Clever Sam, hiring long-hairs to flog records to boppers & building predictable theft loss into our wages (mea culpa)
[13]Hancock's *River: the joni letters*, first jazz Grammy in 43 years
[14]Ketil Bjornstad & David Darling, *The River*, etc.

guessy touch-as-touch-can come-as-you-may don't-freak-the-kids
mum's-the-word, ta' Guess Who. Catch-as-Catch-Can caught tail.
What a blast—Armory Show. Pee-cab's succès de scandale. Marcel's
explosion in a shingle factory [15] w/ no hands guns Man Ray

way. Yes. That way.

The right way. Fling or wing it. Jonathan Winters is not Jonathan
Williams (maybe later). Not Johnny slash Edgar. Go slow ma'
flow while we zapped Mothers at the Eddie & Flo Show [16]

---

[15]An Armory Show critic's reaction to Duchamp's *Nude Descending a Staircase*

[16]With acid friends at Massey Hall, TO, Nov 18, 1970 (if we recall)

Robert Kroetsch: Would You Buy a Bruised Lemon from This Poet?

I had a very strong desire
to kiss a lemon.
No one was watching.
I kissed a lemon.

Sketches of a Lemon — Robert Kroetsch *(with nods to Pechinpah, Dylan, Jimi, Trini, Bob Plant, Phil Edmonston)*

I had a very strong desire

for "Beans, Beans" said

double alias Bobby Zee

refried version, juice de limón

to kiss a lemon

dat musical brute

actin' funny, mal du doute

spied a remon tree, vely plitty

No one was watching

you squeeze that lemon

down along the powder keg

way past werder bremen

I kissed a lemon

so how do you broach a kroetsch?

windy carbs float big air

bruised auto, the more you toot

Joanne Kyger: Post-Life

So "existence" never quits,
never began,   never ended
You see in the moment
So sorry it will never be / like this again—

Post Extinction — Joanne Kyger

So "existence" never quits,

that nausea again, that old

chestnut [17]   phenomenol-ogy

an old grey yid [18] preceding

never began,   never ended

we miscalculated Saint Big Bang

by seconds,   or was it

minutes?   maybe eternity?

---

[17] Disturbing memories of Sartre, nearly 50 years out
[18] ITK poster on a THFC message board

you see in the moment

flash… burn out   that post-life

gloss light *between two eternities of darkness* [19]

hold empty freak-out bang bag

So sorry it will never be / like this again—

oh • my • god   shudder, beyond dizzy

"God loves a cheerful giver" [20]

a failing liver   … quiver, shiver

---

[19]Julian Barnes
[20]Another death at Sunday School

Philip Lamantia: Violent Ekstasis

This world of serpents and weeping women
is crushed in the violence
of a swamp large enough to contain
the enormous razorblade of the night

The Enormous Window — Philip Lamantia (*with nods to PL, Breton, Buñuel & co, & Blaser tales)*

This world of serpents and weeping women

mein vassalage of fee-sis [21] fetus & feces

revolvers and nuns feud on a fulcrum serfing

ekstasis, who's back in the day on this?

is crushed in the violence

touched by the marvelous (*savage fruit*

of lunacy) alchemical *blood of the air*

pure psychic automatism lifts up its skirt

[21] *Incidentally Philip Lamantia: A Study of the Poetics of Surrealism* (MA thesis, 1976: super. Blaser, Bowering, Maud, Quartermain)

of a swamp large enough to contain
randy laddies, oh g-a-w-d he spilt this
where they woke, cum stains on teeth
such chatter *driven mad by desire*

the enormous razorblade of the night
slices dices Andalusian girl glazzball this
new way of seeing—incidentally Pip, you
never unzipped my appendicized letter

Hank Lazer: Quick Prognostications

flip witness
hip gnosis
diminished homage
flesh muse

Days "23" — Hank Lazer [22] (*with nods to M. Mann & the gnostics*)

flip witness
flick 'da switch & trick
some wisdom sayings
— ok, your first heresy

hip gnosis
so… blinded by the light
cut loose like a deuce
another runner in the night

diminished homage
like tapinosis, anti
bodies   negative vibe
in material world

[22]Yrs truly referred to (by Susan M. Schultz) as the "Canadian Hank Lazer"; hence a signed book from Hank: *for Stephen—from the American Hank Lazer to the Canadian Hank Lazer—in poetry, in friendship* (HL, the real deal, & then some, south of the border)

flesh muse
valentines, signor Valentinus
'dat spark in the dark
so… hypo thetical

Ron Loewinsohn: The Altitudes of Attitude

Your eyes that drive me to platitudes

. . .

Looking out the window
there's the moon.
& my typewriter

But This — Ron Loewinsohn *(with nods to Spicer, EP, & SB self-referential)*

Your eyes drive me to platitudes

thinking man's friend to a Braut-

igan spice, steering altitudes

out of bromide paper & gas

Looking out the window

nothing but ocean beyond us

tossed off the shoulder attitudes

switchbacks laid out were just preludes

there's the moon

oh no, not that one, disquietude

wistful as Alba's troubadour lip

(rather drive, like, a vulva valley grrl)

& my typewriter

okay, pound it out w/ aptitude

till it hurts, squeal uncle, all

the while eating himself alive

Jackson Mac Low:
Acrostic for an Estranged Daughter

(tailgating a five-liner glosa)

Hegemony daughter of silence
Sentence Clovis remorse jitney Rinpoche
Reader response perspective
Outrage won polyp wattage
Normal cargo weight souped-up runt

from Twenties — Jackson Mac Low *(no nodding… or noodling)*

***H**egemony daughter of silence*
Exploding strains roll dice, this action jack [23] impulse
And spontaneous, systematic chance-gene-
Rated sorta proto hashtag Cabaret Voltaire
Too Cagey my nightmare child, no chance here

***S**entence Clovis remorse jitney Rinpoche*
Icky Sam, fat l'il cloven hoof alt-right sleaze freeze
C U later die neuen Trungpa, say Budder-gater [24] (ho ho)
Krazy wisdom alright, ein five-plug nickel
Drumpf'd off on the bubble, ich bin goodun clerk'd

---

[23]Two action Jackson's jacked & conflated
[24]W.S. Merwin was Ginsberg's "Buddha-gate," says Tom Clark (*Great Naropa Poetry Wars*)

R*eader response*   *perspective*
Execrable fluff'n, so who was that lit crit yokel [25]
Adds his schtick Cowpokes & Injuns blop on est. & rad
More class'n romance, if tory'n grits, main-
Stream v. avants weren't enough already, n'est Paz?

O*utrage won*   *polyp wattage*
FFS who let the fright rite trash in?
Even odds on Xtian fascist biopsy &
Rise of the Dumpster,[26] sick nodes in network polis
Incidentally pipped à la mort with #BackToPoesy?

N*ormal cargo weight*   *souped-up runt*
(blinded by the light, it's a Hugo Ball
hat trick unter der Mac da knife
(nada nada Dada Dada
his daughter would not come home

---

[25]Leslie Fiedler, if we recall?

[26]Incidentally, at time of writing, attended the Reverend Chris Hedges' homily & talk on "Christian Fascists & the Rise of Donald Trump"

Steve McCaffery: Post-Ubu Roi

(D.G. Jones glosa glancingly revisited)

the tilde ©

the smooth pneuma ©

"I wandered lonely as a cloud"

angular frequency in degrees ©

A Theory of the Lyric © — Steve McCaffery

the tilde ©

yah, copy-rite that ăden-ŏidal twang

choke choker, post-lyrical assault accent

dem valley grrl & bhoy breath bites

the smooth pneuma ©

holy ghosts glide in, at best late [27]

pneumatology strictly (pre-) pre-millennial

tranSports like elevatored smooth jazz

[27]Post-Q, circa Luke—another late developing "myth"

"I [like] wandered lonely as a cloud"

ze (like) floated 71 pronoun non-binary two-spirit

collect prizes awards #OfficialVerseCulture [28] ©

coercively AGAB [29] consumable product

angular frequency in degrees ©

tilt angle, reassign yr frequency, light yr antenna

trans-scribe third-gender one percent ™

Big Pharma open-flush mega donor PAC ®

[28]Or as Charles Bernstein puts it, "the official verse culture enforcers (OVCEs)…"

[29]Or CAGAB: Coercively Assigned Gender At Birth (for those who are not apers of neo-groupthink)

Barry McKinnon: Deep Throat Local Radio Time Signalling

you've got 55 seconds
to come out & see what
you've
won.

Bayday (from *The the.)* — Barry McKinnon

you've got 55 seconds

to hoover the goods

to flash your Rob't Coover maid•en•hoods

to gnaw down on your groover maneuver

to come out & see what

your gag reflex hooks like

your deep throat cooks like

your consummate consumer schnooks like

you've

got 10 'til *The the* then, zen

got 5 & an official verse culture dime

got zero left for fun with slime

won.
(zilch) nothing.
at.
all.

David Meltzer: Gone Beater

When I was a Poet
Everything was a Revelation
no detail less than Cosmic

When I was a Poet

When I was a Poet — David Meltzer *(with nods to D.M., Abbie Hoffman, Ginsberg, Sanders, et al)*

When I was a Poet

on a reverse Abbie H steal at City Lights

an agitprop book installation [30] w/out much

enter or prizing, & no Peace Eyes here…

Everything was a Revelation

'cept 4 "defanged cuddly types like Maynard G

Krebs" digging your six-wing [31] Serpent Power [32]

fry our misspent powdered egg blues mama [33]

---

[30]See *High Maintenance*, p. 22
[31]Revelation 4.8
[32]DM's psychedelic rock band (w/ Clark Coolidge)
[33]See "Egg Blues" in *Rolling Stone*, #105, March 30, 1972, p. 60

no detail less than Cosmic

incl. line-out wrote for yrs truly

on ~~*David's*~~ *Copy*, so sweet of you

hep to head mano a mano

When I was a Poet

at young Beat poet truly yrs was a lone

T.V. Baby Dobie Gillis poet trailing

a slow beater incidentally worth bah…

John Newlove: Lyric, the Lying Poem [34] (a double-barreled glosa)

Then, if I cease desiring,
you may sing a song
of how young I was.
You may praise famous moments

Then, If I Cease Desiring — John Newlove *(with an enterprising nod to Un/Wired* [35]*)*

Then, if I cease desiring

Misread a John Newlove line

then, if I *cleanse*

desiring

You may allow me moments

misread a poet's self-hatred?

It's the *world* is terrible

its un-lyrical shape

you may sing a song

If I did that,

what next

What generic

not monuments, I being

beyond confessional …

pukey suicidal

smarm [36]

---

[34]Phrase from George Bowering's essay on John Newlove, in *A Way With Words*, p. 130
[35]Stephen Bett's poem "Possible Uses for Uric Acid," in *Un/Wired*, p. 83
[36]The phrase "pukey suicidal" confessional poets, from GB's essay, p. 134

of how young I was

antiseptic

eruption

What putrescence

content, it is little

a cork in Heraclitan water

weathering the swarm, long

continual argument [37]

You may praise famous moments

kept in check

— peeing on a

wounded heart

but it is little enough

kept in check

— peed on a

wounded

heart

[37]See Robert McTavish's introduction to Newlove's *A Long Continual Argument*, p. 12

bpNichol: these are my words

i look at you this way
noun then verb
these are my words
I sing to you

song for saint ein — bpNichol *(with nods to Stein, of course, & to Zukofsky; with back nods to Davey & Scobie; & an enterprising nod to* Nota Bene: A Journey [38]*)*

i look at you this way

her voice in my head al-

most 50 years, infectious

… like yesterday

noun then verb

St. Able deferring… if he

told her would she like it,

what history teaches

[38]Stephen Bett, *Nota Bene: A Journey*

these are my words

"Joe in the old coach house on Walmer"

that v. same one, Hey Joe! where you goin'

down Kendal that ol' map in your hand [39]

i sing to you

"a song / entirely in my head" [40]

comme l'amour

in its moment [41]

---

[39] This very coach house sat right smack in the back between Walmer Rd & our old 83A Kendal Ave, in "the Annex" (Toronto). I was too young for McCaffery & nichol's TRG, but old enough for a few nichol dinners at the Miki's a few years later

[40] Zukofsky, "To my wash-stand"

[41] These last two lines from *Nota Bene: A Journey*, p. 37

Frank O'Hara: I love Reverdy for saying yes

I am not a painter, I am a poet.
Why? I think I would rather be
a painter, but I am not. Well,

. . .

I see Mike's painting, called SARDINES.

Why I Am Not a Painter — Frank O'Hara *(with nods to "Lucy Kent XIX"*[42]*, Schuyler, Ashbery & Don Allen)*

I am not a painter, I am a poet.
I do this I do that, I would rather be a jazzer
play Tord G, Colin V [43] ... *while she whispered*
along the keyboard and everyone stopped breathing [44]

Why? I think I would rather be
Abstract Express'ist, Post-Painterly Abs'ist
intimate yeller at New York a.k.a. 10th St School
I suspect he is making a distinction / well who isn't

---

[42]Stephen Bett, *Cruise Control*

[43]Tord Gustavsen, Colin Vallon

[44]Each buoyant, joyfully insouciant (& acerbic) stanza-ending line here, from O'H, is a personal favourite. Plenty of faves to go around though—at least one for every conceivable reader of O'H, & the inconceivable, & unconceivable, ones too.

a painter, but I am not. Well,
so French, & puzzling (never v. sanguine abt pub'ing)
so Camp Urbane, ah such personistic insouciance
you just go on your nerve (all the way fr. Yugen)

I see Mike's painting, called SARDINES
habits of actual speech… the measure of
a continuous attention [45] … *I love Reverdy*
for saying yes, though I don't believe it

[45]Quoting William Navero's bang on definition of "Personism" re: Creeley's voice, from Navero's essay in the Creeley issue of *Boundary 2*, spring/fall, 1978, p.351

Charles Olson: Ate Down to Baby Letters

colored pictures
of all things to eat: dirty / postcards
And words, words, words

. . .

No eyes or ears left

The Songs of Maximus — Charles Olson *(with nods to D.G. Jones glosa, Dylan, Ginsberg, & Phil Spector)*

colored pictures

read forward / back, dizzy mu-sick

dis fury 'n gurry,[46] gutted

sick muse [47] oceanside us

of all things to eat: dirty / postcards

dat capital obs-kenity: [48] Mad Ave shrinkage [49]

---

[46]Bett, "Lift Off 10: bite size (after Olson): Was it gurry/or offal//A bird at sea,/surely"
[47]"mu-sick, the sick music and muse": Sherman Paul, *Olson's Push*, p. 126
[48]"advertising men are the worst kind of obscenity": Frank Davey, PhD thesis: *Theory and Practise in the Black Mountain Poets*, p. 240
[49]The vast majority of Madison Ave payroll, evidently, is taken up by outsourced psychologists (not copy-writers, etc.). So much for advertising as "informational."

what is said,[50] like Big O Tyres ate down

to baby letters (ad-verbs galore

And words, words, words

all dis palaver (don'tcha, Mr. Jones?

bomb bard-bard-bard-ment

invaded, appropriated, outraged

… *starving hysterical naked* (too

No eyes or ears left

even dose crude instruments [51]

even muzak long gone fr. ma' town

even dat spector, lulled, no wall

of sound left, eez all pop'd

---

[50]Chas Olson, of course, on the unfortunate shift from *muthos* (mouth) to *logos* (reason), curtesy dose Greeks; mu-sick & muzak: "what is said is sick, a sick story from a sick mouth": Robert von Hallberg, *Charles Olson: The Scholar's Art*, p. 58

[51]"the mu-sick of the juke box has made the ear a crude instrument": Paul Christensen, *Charles Olson: Call Him Ishmael, p.* 123

Joel Oppenheimer: A Luggage Tag

in the seat / of a car
like teenagers
. . .
what were we
dreaming of

At Fifty — Joel Oppenheimer *(with a nod to Miker Mike)*

in the seat / of a car

a fave bit of ephemera, this

poem printed on luggage tag

hung out with its spine-meister

like teenagers

from a loop of twine

tied up to ship well into

this far flung future

what were we

at fifty— if Joel were alive he would

love your new book of poems,

just the kind he championed [52]

dreaming of

our kind & kindred champ

well tagged at the Poetry Project

you Take-a-Bow-Airy, maestro

---

[52]A back cover blurb by M.G. (Mike) Stephens

Ron Padgett: Adventures of a Sleight'd Hand

Beautiful / an O fell from
your mouth into the
letters L V and E
spelling out LVEO

The Adventures of Mr and Mrs Jim [Dine] and Ron [Padgett]
— Ron Padgett *(with plenty nods to these earlier glosas)*

Beautiful / an O fell from
the sleight'd hand of Mr Jim Dine
Oh it's been such a lone song time
oh ahh that long held hero of mine

your mouth into the
juicy grape-load on dat blackberry vine
4' ever beyon' description stuck in brine
hangin tough, this last piece of twine

letters L V and E
thud up an aveolar lateral sign
isolate, u labiodental fricative swine
silent E's… love's adenoidal whine

spelling out LVEO
a 1 & ah' 2 tapinosis, his poet ore-fill'd mine
tap to hip gnosis thru an old *Z* zine [53]
evol cover'd [54] from St Ein to Franz Kline

53Kenward Elmslie's *Z Press* & Z *Magazine*
[54]bpNichol's concrete/visual poem "evol": full front cover image, *love: a book of remembrances*

Tom Pickard: Oop norf, fook sake

bulimia oblivia
   I
[h] ate
   it

bulimia oblivia — Tom Pickard *(w/ nods to Basil Bunting, the Newcastle poets, Liverpool "beat" poets, George Harrison, bpNichol)*

bulimia oblivia

don't woof yr cookies (Newcastle Brown Ale)

purge yourself, sunflower

say somebody's lil' bunting

   I

here's I me mine in yr eye

oop norf, fook sake, you bet

Yorks Bete beat the Pool [55]

---

[55] *Piers Plowman*, first "lit" (up) instance of the family name Bete/Bett/Betts, with all its variant early spellings

[h] ate

not to get all cocky

h'8 no 'aitch 4 bp concrete

viz, getting all visual

it

ate me ('arf-time) so don't be

telling porkies, pie-head

magpie caught in a barcode [56]

[56]Newcastle United Football Club nicknames: Magpies, Barcodes

Jeremy Prynne: Paratactic Procedures

Here I saw… telescopic to the field inside the mouth
where speech parts of separation had been swallowed
in foreground… fricative was the advice and
to palate by adhesion said to be forward

Kazoo Dreamboats — Jeremy Prynne *(with a nod to Gerald Bruns* [57]*)*

Here I saw… telescopic to the field inside the mouth

chokeberries on the line rotten beyond description

chomp by field ate down to baby letter shivers, bottle

our mal du doute upchuck trick, there's a good chap

where speech parts of separation had been swallowed

by black holes, do not interrupt his moment of disconnect

at all / anyway / whatever / even so / rubbish [58]

goes down whoosh it's got some teeth in it

---

[57]See Gerald Bruns' essay on Prynne's *Kazoo Dreamboats,* in Bruns, *Interruptions: The Fragmentary Aesthetic in Modern Literature*
[58]Complete (untitled) poem in Prynne's *Down where changed*

in foreground… fricative was the advice and

couple disjunct blimeys in a row pick & prune a'miss

near scurvy them ballsy labiodental f'n fearsome

feckful avant swine, dey do dis da joint

to palate by adhesion said to be forward

by outward tastes like collage glued on the tongue

you can only "be" in the moment, just out *Near/Miss* [59]

meets Gordon Lish meets Lewis Black, well done old son

[59]Charles Bernstein's *Near/Miss*

Raymond Queneau: Fa'der of Oulipo

brownwaters, blackwaters, wonderwaters
seawaters, oceanwaters, flashingwaters
brighten the night, nighten the day
songs Sunday to Saturday

Les Ziaux — Raymond Queneau *(with a nod & a wink & a thx to P. Simon, for the chops)*

brownwaters, blackwaters, wonderwaters

wanderlust of an unrestrained M. Oulipo

pataphysical swat team walling off imaginary

solutions, constrain-eyed zone-outs

seawaters, oceanwaters, flashingwaters

lightning over troubled waters ('friend' indeed)

sail on silver girl, syrup strained & stained

oh it's double trouble now sunshine, capital Ds & Ts

brighten the night, nighten the day

lighten up all the bars on Oulipan way [60]

oh when darkness comes (runnin' around)

put a glose spell on you— Restraint!

songs Sunday to Saturday

bridge to lay me down, so rough

when time chops weary sea thru sea, too tough

you will be unconstrained, that gap in the fence

[60]Oulipo law: "A text written according to a constraint describes the constraint."

Tom Raworth: gifted

a present
that
fits me
to a t

Ace — Tom Raworth *(with a nod to old Stones… & stoners)*

a present

gifted, & at arms (rah-rah)

shabby old cardigan, slippers, &c. [61]

— the real raw deal!

that

's worth a lotta r…

She corrects [62] / x-ray

muse in my devices

---

[61] TR's reading at Kootenay School of Writing, mid-'90s

[62] Rae Armantrout corrects my pronunciation, over dinner: Rāworth, not Răworth, as I'd been saying, like, for-ever…

fits me

sting or other wrays

Rae-worth, Raw-worth let's call

the whole thing off ?

to a t

Om boy… pleased to meet'cha

full steam a head

top speed, them ol' rollers [63]

---

[63]TR's break-neck, monotone reading speed—bravura performance

D.C. Reid: Riffing a Line from PK

and so, forgettable, and so forgot.
Think language to woo, an onslaught
of song, a medium of exchange, so
we might barter, heckle with hot

Language Games (a glosa poem) — D.C. Reid *(with nods to PK & all poets at 15)*

and so, forgettable, and so forgot. [64]

th' da landed i shy & shier (spicy wasp soup?)

blocks from home, out of this world

paged to a wisp, Mexicano curios [65]

Think language to woo, an onslaught

Tu-whit tu-whoo, a merry note (eh olé)

enthrall'd to po-etry's sullen art

tap'd his foot, dis dancer doyenne

---

[64]Dennis Reid's glossed line is from PK Page's poem "The gold sun"
[65]PK & her husband, da's diplomat friend, had just returned home from Mexico

of song, a medium of exchange, so

forgot, waylaid, riff'd-upon-Ripon [66]

this danse russe shaman *uta* dat house [67] ?

song'n dance man into da glosa

we might barter, heckle with hot

press'd flame-outs unforgettable

fire enough blanks, gloss over

this mazy life by now

[66]PK's Ripon Road house just a couple of blocks from the childhood home
[67]WCW's "Danse Russe": "happy genius of my household"; etym: protective spirit of the sleeping household; *uta*: original Japanese term for poetry (literally: "song")

Monty Reid: Contributors' Notes

Monty Reid always reads the contributors' notes first. Before he even looks at the rest of the magazine. He has become interested in how people imagine themselves. Perhaps he has come to believe that these notes are more dynamic, more provocative, more disturbing even, than the poems.

Contributors' Notes — Monty Reid *(with nods to both Capilano & Malahat Reviews)*

Monty Reid always reads the contributors' notes first. Before he even

accepts submissions exclusively from women, trans, nonbinary, Two-Spirited,

and genderqueer/gender nonconforming writers, multidisciplinary artists and

creative facilitators whose pronouns have been longlisted for their *entire life*

while Most of Canada is putting the burn on women, queer and poc voices [68]

looks at the rest of the magazine. He has become interested in how

his eponymous clothing label examines dress through Indigenous perspectives

on gender, queerness, and ancestral knowledge on unceded territories of the

Musquem and Tsleil-Waututh First Nations (colonially-known-as-Vancouver)

[68]Line from a personal email from an Ontario publisher enthusing about current Canadian publishing opportunities. Expect the acronym LGBTQ12S to grow exponentially, fueled by neofascist groupthink.

people imagine themselves. Perhaps he has come to believe that these

"Hot Damn It's A Queer Slam" Two-Spirit and Nonbinary poets are voracious consumers of gender-fluid hybridized comic books of mixed settler descent raised on Treaty 1 and 9 Territories in Manitoba and northern Ontario

notes are more dynamic, more provocative, more disturbing even, than the poems

that explore the intersectionalities of identity, belonging, and storytelling among queer newcomers to Canada, as told to queer, transfemme Latinx poets from Santa Cruz who know where the time goes, it flows to da' ze [69]

[69]As does the white noise of arts' money. First there was the LIP grant generation, now it's Flip Gen.

Michael Rothenberg: And Millennial Prizes for All

I want to win a Pulitzer prize. For something
Poetry. Fiction. It doesn't matter I want a reward
Otherwise, I will only exist in the pages of some weird anthology
Buried in the archives of a university library

Unhurried Vision — Michael Rothenberg

I want to win a Pulitzer prize. For something

glee filled, self-fraught, faux-hysteric, smart

alecky as MR's sweet-beat heart on your sleeve

no bully-bully nouveau PoWorld fakes & flakes [70]

Poetry. Fiction. It doesn't matter I want a reward

make it a primer, mano, a 'how to' score PKs diving [71]

in the box … a go slow pro-mo at the show-po

[70]Careerist poets win prizes. See Brian Fawcett's article "Why Sharon Thesen Doesn't Win Poetry Prizes" (*Capilano Review*, Spring, 2008): Thesen's neither over-earnest nor shameless, she doesn't kiss up, & her poems don't sound like "machines." And note previous glosa's header to see how 'swamped' Cap Review has become in the ten short years to the present—from avant journal to PC capitulated mainstream

[71]Pardon the puns: PK Page glosa, penalty kicks

When I was a Poet [72] too, hoho, those poseur-stuffed ninnies

Otherwise, I will only exist in the pages of some weird anthology

Best in Show, tuckered out tropes for earnest folks (& dopes) mousey

marketeer awards galore, check your pronoun trick at hum-drummies

craven divers box to box press Mina Loy's toys & gender-bender boys [73]

Buried in the archives of a university library

down with breathless poet voicings po'tree prize readers [74]

oh mano, I feel another L. Black harrumph careen by, whoopsie!

I love Reverdy for saying yes, though I don't believe it either [75]

---

[72]See earlier David Meltzer glosa (for whom MR generously 'cared', as he did for Philip Whalen at the end of his life)

[73]Whoops, more puns, at boxer/poet Arthur Craven, Mina Loy, Creeley's Divers Press, &c.

[74]The infamous "poetry reading *voice*": rimes with cocktail hour's "piano *stylings*..." And see Fawcett article again: prize-winning poets & their "self-declarative puke we call poetry readings." John Wieners coined an even more colourful term for these ninnies: "puke suckers" (JW reading at the 92nd St "Y," NYC, decades ago).

[75]See earlier Frank O'Hara glosa

Aram Saroyan: Six Minimal Pieces, in Thirds (a tri-columnar glosa, or two-door glosa with side door)

fall over	*all all*	*eyeye*
fall over	*all all*	*o r*
fall over	*ly ly*	*o r*
fall over	*ly ly*	*YOU YOU*

Six from Complete Minimal Poems — Aram Saroyan *(with nods to Duncan McNaughton, Victor Coleman & The Kingsmen, & The Left Banke kiddo)*

fall over	*all all*	*eyeye*
And	hot press	Louie Lou-aye [76]
when	Duncan	whoa
I	McNaughton [77]	no

fall over	*all all*	*o r*
see	chap	me
the	beyond	gotta
sign	lovely	go

[76]Victor Coleman riffing on stage with Louis Zukofsky's name, Vancouver Poetry Centre, 1979 (author of Canadian version, *Eh* ?)

[77]*Somewhere In The Stream*, chapbook (Blue Press, 2019)

fall over

that

points

one

y ly

wry

arch

sardonic

o r

hey baby

they

pronouns

fall over

way…

walks

away

ly ly

hip wit

right in

the guts

YOU YOU

go

one

way

now

Peter Schjeldahl: Nostalgic Ode from Post-Age

Vietnam / Drugs / Civil Rights / Rock… the blows of history
That have left my generation
Its peculiar battered silhouette
Face it, we haven't produced much

My Generation — Peter Schjeldahl *(with nods to Joni Mitchell & The Who)*

Vietnam / Drugs / Civil Rights / Rock… the blows of history

a touch too young to raise a pentagon

touch less hex a gone come of age

the man Sam speeding on Yonge St. [78]

That have left my generation

m-my g-g-generation, yakety-yak

forever hung on wrap talk, that *billion year*

old carbon, a dig now dug, sold plumb up

[78]Long-hairs flogging vinyl at Sam the Record Man's flagship store

Its peculiar battered silhouette

flame's out… hero dust to stardust blue too

is the hero, ditch outside Oswego NY

a year late, dreamt he'd never be bonded [79]

Face it, we haven't produced much

— okay, but you copped the best career move [80]

(ditto a not-too-shabby Bill Berkson)

"Cover art by Joe Brainard," of course

---

[79]A couple of titles here: Tom Pickard's *Hero Dust*, Bill Berkson's *Blue Is the Hero*. And overnight in a ditch about a year to the day after Woodstock, dreamed a failure poem

[80]Libbie Rifkin, *Career Moves*, with chapters on Olson, Creeley, Zukofsky, Berrigan. (Schjehdahl's career move as art critic/reviewer was perhaps the best move of all.)

Gary Snyder: Riffs on a Trippy Zenny Poem

on a wobbling speck
a big rock weathered funny
this dream pops. it was real;
and it lasted forever.

For a Stone Girl at Sanchi — Gary Snyder *(with a nod to Joni again)*

on a wobbling speck

runny trippy, zen as now

blowing / peaking us away that

bear-shit-on-the-trail school [81]

a big rock weathered funny

stoner girl, planet earth

muscle tone [82] deep ecology, spaced

out cycles for…ever (shudder)

[81]As snidely said of Snyder, Whalen, Welch (& Rexroth too)
[82]Allen Graves, "A Look at Gary Snyder" (*TISH newsletter, no. 10,*1962): "we have these two qualities in Snyder… a sensual delight in movement of muscles and sounds, and a sense of progressions, of continuities."

this dream pops. it was real;

it was spacey / the real deal

re-imagined, irreparable,[83] back in

a garden wrong side of grass

and it lasted forever.

plenty agora freak-outs to go round

fly a starship thru, no *raison* here

just the eye of the needle [84]

[83]Just released Robin Blaser biography: the "Irreparable" is foundational, as was "the Real" in our '70s grad school.

[84]Excuse school French. Also, can't recall which of the progressive theologists notes "*camel* through the eye of a needle" is a mistranslation for "raison," which tells a pretty fruitful story.

Jack Spicer: No One Listens to Poetry

No one listens to poetry. The ocean
Does not mean to be listened to. A drop

• • •

It pounds the shore. White and aimless signals. No
One listens to poetry.

Language — Jack Spicer *(with nods to Robin Blaser)*

No one listens to poetry. The ocean

rolls over us — *these* coastal people

nothing's out beyond this last gasp edge [85]

serial decoder of breakers

Does not mean to be listened to. A drop

drip drip on little green transceivers, whatever [86]

---

[85]I've often quoted the following lines (born to it, so to speak). Spicer: "We are a coast people. / There is nothing but ocean out beyond us. We grasp / The first thing coming." ("Ten Poems for Downbeat"). And Robin Blaser's essay on Spicer, "The Practise of Outside": Spicer's west coast landscape "seems to be at the edge of something, a gated place, an end which opens again."

[86]Speaking of this, in astrophysics the developing LGM theory (LGM1, LGM2, etc.) is a physicists' in-joke (Little Green Men 1, 2, etc.). Martin Rees, *Before the Beginning: Our Universe and Others*

comes in from that darkness around us [87]

you were the real outsider, honest angel

It pounds the shore. White and aimless signals. No

jolts or jive, so okay dictate something, anything…

Nothing, you said, *Deserves to live*

& I heard that, crystal clear

One listens to poetry.

It's difficult to get the news [88]

No one listens to radio anymore,

not even Martians

---

[87]Blaser biographer, Miriam Nichols, on the subject of RB's (& JS's) "serial" poems: "the idea of seriality…it's what comes into the space…in the poem" (Nichols' interview with Paul Nelson, *Splabman*, Jan 13, 2020). And this vital bit of news from Spicer on "serial" poems: "Poems should echo and reecho against each other. They should create resonances. They cannot live alone any more than we can." And of course the echo of Creeley's "the darkness surrounds us."

[88]WCW's well known lines: "It is difficult / to get the news from poems / yet men die miserably every day / for lack / of what is found there."

Richard Stevenson: White and Airless Signals

(for Rick)

It was the pulse I was interested in.
Getting between those interstices of being.
But without a constant of normality
I could neither transmit nor receive.

Mike's Acid Story — Richard Stevenson *(with nods to Jack Spicer & Robert Herrick)*

It was the pulse I was interested in.

White and airless signals,[89] a radio no one

listens to anymore (trans'istors) the night

they drove ol' anti-cedents down

Getting between those interstices of being.

The old lightbulb trick, as told by an ex + poet-

star-grrl, couple high school acid queens

day trippers all along the graveyard shift

[89]Phrase from Spicer—see previous glosa.

But without a constant of normality

no can check yr stoned pronouns at the space

ship door, w-a-y out b'yond those edgy

coastal folk (oh decoder of serial breakers)

I could neither transmit nor receive.

Such a dumb numb cisgender, transceiver bust

… so gather ye zies & zems while ye may

dose psychic authorities [90] will have zeir day

[90]Lawrence Ferlinghetti coined the phrase "psychic authoritarianism," as I recall, for New Agers; reviving the phrase for mind-bending third-gendering folk seems likewise appropriate nowadays.

Sharon Thesen: North Shore Scrawl

My car I drive back & forth
around the town over bridges & here
and there, like everyone else
driving their cars. In the back seat

I Drive the Car — Sharon Thesen *(with numerous nods to Ed Dorn)*

My car I drive back & forth

road-testing the language, one hand tied to the wheel [91]

the other transcribes white signal scrawl

Drive, he sd, you'd never sound like a machine [92]

around the town over bridges & here

my town (bubble trouble city) proverbial back of the

hand, every bridge, crossing, laps water, 2nd Narrows

bridge each day / needle / tree sails past the Rez [93]

91Ed Dorn talks about road-testing (& strumming) the language, reading & writing in a scrawled hand while driving, which requires alertness to say the least. See Dorn's *Interviews, Documents for New Poetry 1, Hello La Jolla, Yellow Lola* (*section 101*), & his lecture at the Kerouac School of Disembodied Poetics, *Talking Poetics from Naropa Institute, Vol. One*.
92From Creeley's exemplary "I Know a Man" (see Creeley glosa), & from Fawcett's essay on Thesen—see footnote to Michael Rothenberg glosa..
93Burrard Band, Chief Dan, then Leonard, George—good neighbours.

and there, like everyone else

reading, writing on the road (microbial alert)

strumming the language, stitching the poem

riff / riffing / rift endless yellowed note pads

driving their cars. In the back seat [94]

torn pictures (Tweed Curtains[95]) — the common duty

of the poet in an era of onslaught upon alertness [96]

scrawl, scrabble the good bacteria of language [97]

---

[94]See Oppenheimer glosa: "what were we dreaming of"?
[95]Oak Bay (suburb of Victoria), home to Brit ex-pats living in an Edwardian "Old Country" that never quite was.
[96]Dorn's *Yellow Lola* (p. 63): "The common duty of the poet / in this era of massive dysfunction / & generalized onslaught upon alertness / is to maintain the plant..."
[97]Thesen, in *The Capilano Review* (3.5, The Sharon Thesen Issue), frontispiece: "...poetry being the good bacteria of language..."

Orchid Tierney: Exaptation to Bipedalism

(for O)

i suck
back two
bruised syll
ables

brachiation — Orchid Tierney *(with nods to Wiki & PRRB)* [98]

i suck

at most

forms of bra

chiation

back two

brachiators slinging

parsed sentences in

splintered shards

[98]The Oulipo trick here is to restrict the poem to the wording from two limited sources: Wiki, on "brachiation," & my own blurb & review of Tierney's chapbook *Ocean Plastic*, in the *Pacific Rim Review of Books*.

bruised syll

able to brachiate one's

living praxis of mish

mashed phrases

ables

to chop and change whip

like generative lang

uage globs

Tom Veitch: *I never give you my pillow*

Boy, you're gonna carry that weight,
a long time.
in a monster climate of words
and slow paranoia.

Worst Storm — Tom Veitch *(with a nod to Lennon & McCartney)*

Boy, you're gonna carry that weight,

& it aint none like Covid-19, lite as a

microbe *yeh yeh yeh* (pop quiz:

I wanna… rimes Richard Bona)

a long time

since *Death College* [99] brother, aint heavy

it's my language po'lice trans zirself

Tom's FB tells us gloss Violi too! [100]

[99]Title of the Veitch book from which this poem proceeds.
[100]In reply to my FB post that I can't decide which "V" poet to gloss (Veitch or Violi) Veitch springs up & types "Paul Violi was a great man," & then he promotes Bill Zavatsky too, who in turn also springs up on my timeline.

in a monster climate of words

da Trumper presser cons Reality TV

(hey *T*om *V*eitch) #RallyDatBase [101]

amuse ourselves to death (ahh...) [102]

and slow paranoia.

soma' deez peeps too 'tupid

2B fit to terror, left us not

surreal, not even *un*real [103]

---

[101]Trump, aka Blubber-Boy (see *Un/Wired*, p.66), plays the TV ratings game with his press briefings on coronavirus pandemic, brags he's outperforming Monday Night NFL as hundreds of thousands (so far) suffocate to death.

[102]Neil Postman, *Amusing Ourselves to Death.*

[103]It's cliché, almost caricature, nowadays to say something's "surreal" when meaning "unreal."

Paul Violi: Pork Chops

Big Daddy
Walk in the park, day bright and fair,
Flip a cripple a nickel,
Kick a pigeon in the air.

Big Daddy — Paul Violi *(with nods all over, gladly)*

Big Daddy

-O's dialing up Giorno Poetry Systems [104]

for latest State directives: *Appropriate Termin-*

ology / Guidelines for Inclusive Curriculum [105]

Walk in the park, day bright and fair,

sing out / tune in w/ the TADs (& Dads) [106]

[104]And not to forget John Giorno's *Dial-a-Poem*
[105]See "High-Maintenance" in *High-Maintenance*, p. 25
[106]TAD: Temporarily-Able-Bodied (you're living on borrowed time, bro); & *Tads* & Dads (poetry magazine, & its mentors, ed., Jamie Reid, et al)

tap tap that tapinosis track — "it just seems

the pork chop and is ugly" [107]

Flip a cripple a nickel,

— whoopsie, *person with* for gawd sake!

are you, like, linguistically

challenged or like *what*?

Kick a pigeon in the air

in the glossolalia of glossopoeisis [108] — add

back-tongue (cleft) to our vaunted avants

Veitch's law: *Paul Violi was a great man* (period)

[107]See *Sass 'n Pass,* pp, 66-7: Freshman college comp class student 'production', eg., 1: "Unless he is obeyed his uncle or his aunt mechanically, it just seems the pork chop and is ugly"; eg., 2: "Albee has written a cleaver play" (chop); eg., 3: that dude Meursault… "He killed the man, not with anger or hatred but simply with a gun."
[108]As opposed to glossoptosis (cleft tongue); *Glossolalia Journal,* #12, Finland; glossopoeisis (see Adeena Karasick, *ÆROTOMANIA*, excerpted by both X-periBlogspot.com & League of Canadian Poets, Apr 20/20)

Fred Wah: A Floating Space

nv s ble
tr ck
five 6 seven nine and ten
its a trap. [109]

Pictograms from the Interior of B.C. — Fred Wah *(with nods to Creeley's numbers)*

nv s ble

naught for the eyes

behind any danse's russe [110]

a floating space (no axes

tr ck

trans-ekphrastic,[111] no dots

to connect, no juiced up

berries in this vine-line

---

[109]"Its" [sic]
[110]Once again in these glosas, WCW's renowned & wonderful poem, as a self-portrait; look at all the i's
[111]Bowering notes Wah's response to these pre-historic cave drawings is "transcreative"—neither translations nor descriptions." (Intro to Wah's *Selected*, p. 15)

five 6 seven nine and ten

by the numbers then One and

one and one / Make a picture

two things / one and one [112]

rolls back into itself (… but

its a trap.

Trompe l'oeil frame(d) / two things,

four things / one and three [113]

this dream pops too, rubble freed

[112]"One and one… a picture" (from Creeley's "Enough"); "two things one and one" (from Creeley's "Song (What do you want, love")

[113]"two and two…one and three" (from Creeley's "Numbers"); & more loveliness still: "let / me sing, *one* to / *one* to *one*, and let / me follow" (from Creeley's "One thing done")

Lewis Warsh: Dancing Up a Ruse

Rousseau said something about something.
He said something.
He said:[114] *I'm going to give you a fat lip.*
The doorman held the umbrella

Superficial Things — Lewis Warsh *(with nods to L.W. & Un/Wired)*[115]

Rousseau said something about something.

My father shortened his name from Warshafsky

when he was in his twenties. Maybe it was

2 a.m. at Anne & Lewis's, which is one for the money old son

He said something.

Pepper told me he was gay on the

train from Boston to New York.

One track / One ticket / One way

---

[114] Sic

[115] This glosa is almost entirely a collage, or pastiche (or mash-up), of two Lewis Warsh poems, glossed lines from the Berrigan & Prynne glosas, & a minimalist poem from *Un/Wired* featuring an epigraph from a Warsh novel.

He said: I'm going to give you a fat lip.

But he didn't say (mid-Atlantic voice)

don't forget to warsh your hands old boy

there's a good chap, the old upchuck trick

The doorman held the umbrella

for the dark figure with the fat lip in the rain

said he was dancing up a ruse to snag a late train

speeding at 4 a.m. trying not to buck your grain, rattle your chain

Phyllis Webb: The Spit

And spit
give me water for spit.
Then give me
a face.

Solitary Confinement [116] — Phyllis Webb

And spit

broken glass

for shards

to speak

give me water for spit.

Gloss this mal du

doute   … never

was spat out

[116] This section of Webb's poem starts, "Let my tongue hang out / to remember the thirst for life. / Let my togue hang out / to deliver itself / of the bitter curd. / And spit / …"

Then give me

ash in time

to witness

its burn

a face.

To spite

itself

still

Lew Welch: Which Planet Are You (Currently) On?

Draw a circle a hundred feet round.
Inside the circle are
300 things nobody understands, and, maybe
nobody's ever really seen.

Step out onto the Planet — Lew Welch *(with nods to earlier glosas)*

Draw a circle a hundred feet round.

Big enough to hold that old

Franz Kline line [117]   … in a forest

of Zen-inflected absence

Inside the circle are

you sitting still?   expecting a tr ck?

Locked in   snug as a bug

(in a toppled chestnut tree

[117]This LW poem is hand-written, in black ink, Zen-like calligraphy—at the top of which a simply lovely oval-ish circle, looking also like a deft Franz Kline drawing.

300 things nobody understands, and, maybe

one twins another, this freedom bit

that satori hit

& which dream pops first

nobody's ever really seen.

It's voided (ha)   shudder / quiver / shiver

Step out onto another planet   far side of

despair, don't hang there for long [118]

---

[118]Sartre: "Life begins on the other side of despair"—where existential freedom & Zen awakening too briefly meet & hang out.

Philip Whalen: Vernacular Drift

I praise those ancient Chinamen
Who left me a few words,
Usually a pointless joke or a silly question
* * *
& konked out among the busted spring rain cherryblossom winejars

Hymnus Ad Patrem Sinensis — Philip Whalen *(with more nods to PW)*

I praise those ancient Chinamen

dose old vernaculars key is *praise* so no shoot …

first's the big ask ahh Zen monk(ery) lovely man!

bits of sugar-blossom in his beard [119]

Who left me a few words,

a *continuous fabric (nerve movie?)*

Bald and pink and great

This is a man you could love [120]

---

[119] This & other italicized lines from this & other PW poems.
[120] These two lines from Michael Rothenberg's journal poem *Unhurried Vision*, written while MR was caregiver to a bravely dying Philip Whalen. MR's stanza continues, "And the poetry he makes/can jump out the window/and get away fast"

Usually a pointless joke or a silly question

(*If You're So Smart, Why Ain't You Rich?*)

Anybody (quote) who doesn't love & admire

~~Allen Ginsberg~~ [Philip Whalen] is an asshole [121]

& konked out among the busted spring rain cherryblossom winejars

Zen Cowboys [122] take a load off *clink clink clink clank clink*

Sinologists spank ol' Fenollosa, the five character shift [123]

Happy to have saved us all [!]

---

[121]Ed Sanders said this about Ginsberg, in Sanders' novel *Shards of God.*
[122]Dale Smith (of *Skanky Possum* fame) quoting Ron Silliman on Whalen & Dorn.
[123]See "Three characters," in *Lucy Kent & other poems.*

John Wieners: Inc. & Non (or, The Poem's in the Footnote)

Charles Olson	*Jack Spicer*	*Fred Wah*	*William Everson*
Ed Dorn	*Robert Creeley*	*Joel Oppenheimer*	*Phyllis Webb*
Jonathan Williams	*Gary Snyder*	*Joanne Kyger*	*Paul Blackburn*
Frank O'Hara	*Philip Whalen*	*Phillip Lamantia*	*Ted Berrigan*

Poets I Have Met [124] — John Wieners

Charles Olson	*Jack Spicer*	*Fred Wah*	*William Everson*
Denise Levertov	Bill Berkson	Anne Waldman	Victor Coleman
Robin Blaser	Kenneth Koch	Lewis MacAdams	Herbert Hunke
Barbara Guest	John Ashbery	Helen Adam	Jack Micheline
Ed Dorn	*Robert Creeley*	*J. Oppenheimer*	*Phyllis Webb*
James Schuyler	Leroi Jones	Robert Kelly	Roy Kiyooka
Edwin Denby	Gilbert Sorrentino	Michael McClure	John Taggart
Robert Duncan	Ray Bremser	Gregory Corso	Carol Bergé
Jonathan Williams	*Gary Snyder*	*Joanne Kyger*	*Paul Blackburn*
L. Ferlinghetti	Ed Sanders	Diane di Prima	Tony Towle
Bob Kaufman	Harold Dull	Diane Wakosi	Frank Lima
Allen Ginsberg	George Stanley	Rochelle Owens	Vincent Ferrini

[124]In one long, multi-page column John Wieners' poem "Poets I Have Met" names 233 poets he had "met" by the late 1960s. Sixteen of these have been glossed here in *Broken Glosa*; the rest are names that coulda, woulda, shoulda been glossed, given time & space. Seven are fellow Canadians—can you find them? (NB: the publisher's list here actually runs to 228 names & is miscounted as 233, including Bro Antoninus & William Everson counted as two names "met," not one, & incl William Burroughs & Michael Rumaker as "poets." Do not trust [the publisher's] printed word?

Frank O'Hara	*Philip Whalen*	*Philip Lamantia*	*Ted Berrigan*
Peter Orlovsky	Ebbe Borregaard	Richard Brautigan	Larry Fagin
Jack Kerouac	Stan Persky	Jerry Rothenberg	Kenward Elmslie
Dan Zimmerman	Gerald Malanga	Gerrit Lansing	Clayton Eshelman

Joshua Marie Wilkinson: Uppercut Two Shoe

One of those bruisecuts that boxers get.
I want somebody to come over here & punch me in the neck.
Am I on the phone because I can't end this near a bed or a desk or
anything stable enough to fuck on?

Do your friends know you well enough… — Joshua Marie Wilkinson

One of those bruisecuts that boxers get.

Yup, we're boxed in, Dispatch bosses dub dis

careerist poet (dub dub dob) though I don't

believe it, sucker for da kid's skillset (kerplunk) [125]

I want somebody to come over here & punch me in the neck.

S'ok, dis'patched on zee double, one volunteer slap'o Gen Y guy

(& Y not) stamp seal OfficialVerseCulture, I Owe Ya

School of Po-Design … *He* [sooo] *plays in the band Califone*

---

[125] *Dispatches from the Poetry Wars* editor, in a personal email, dubs JMW a "careerist poet"; & don't forget Cubscout careerists: "dyb dyb dob" (Do Your Best, Do Our Best).

Am I on the phone because I can't end this near a bed or a desk or

are we backing Edwardian ennui redux, so lame, *He lives in Chicago*

and Athens, Georgia (yawn) two-slice millennial privilege

artiste arriviste, no grain in dat Whiteboy'um [126]

anything stable enough to fuck on?

cast-yr-couch, off-kilter, cam.obscura polaroids 52 humongous

thank-queues unflagging indefatigable reader ship [127] poetry-

by-committee sign off groovy two shoes in the side ring

[126]A Stan Rice poetry title, *Whiteboy*
[127]Adjectives here from JMW's Iowa Poetry Prize winning *Lug Your Careless Body*'s effusive acknowledgements pages (plural); & *Califone, Chicago, Athens*, above: cool quotes from polaroid closing pages of JMW's *Selenography.*

Jonathan Williams: Polis is Spies

Eighteen months after you left us,
poetry (that abused & discredited substance;
that refuge of untalented snobs, yobs, and bores)
sinks nearer the bottom of the whirling world.

At Brigflatts Burial Ground — Jonathan Williams *(with nods to Olson's eyes & to Bill Lavender)*

Eighteen months after you left us,

full coarse bunting, bambaazled to a fault

& by the sound oop norf, you bet

light airs of music / we are left with [128]

poetry (that abused & discredited substance;

try that bused & credit-edited stance

on someone's else *Try writing a JW poem*

Try to imitate one, try to pass one off... [129]

[128]Jonathan Williams, "The Anchorite," *An Ear in Bartram's Tree*
[129]"Can't be done," concludes Robert Kelly on JW.

that refuge of untalented snobs, yobs, and bores)

that fugue of lent nobs, juiced gobs w/out scores

blue lives that don't matter, these eyes on

polis, politeia, la po-lice fook sake

sinks nearer the bottom of the whirling world

down by the docks, polis is spies in lavender ink [130]

only those unborn to the ur-redneck manner would find

this grotesquerie some sort of kicker,[131] nuff at stake

[130]See Bill Lavender's essay "La Police" (in *ID*) on the origins of Police as private organisations for property protection on the docks, in factories, etc.

[131]JW, journal entry in *Hot What?*

Jeffrey Cyphers Wright: Bullet & Proofed

(for Jeff)

The late Jim Brodey once instructed me
on composing a New York School poem:
"Use blue *and name a couple friends."*
This off-the-cuff take is on-the-button.

Bare Season — Jeff Wright *(with slight nods to Stein & Stones)*

The late Jim Brodey once instructed me

always ride the high octane long-haul on an

uncluttered heart, you'll be bulletproofed

Blue Lyre pants on fire (all the way to Newark) [132]

---

[132] Three brief notes: Andre Codrescu: "I emptied two magazines of my .380 PRK at Jeffrey C. Wright's bulletproof poems, and they didn't make a dent"; Jeff asked yrs truly to proof 'n prune his *Blue Lyre* ms; & decades ago, before Jeff's Hard Press hit hard times (funding), we'd planned on a postcard for my poem "Fire Poem: To Newark," artwork by Denis Lukas. (LeRoi Jones & *Yugen* also from Newark.)

on composing a New York School poem:

Here's the deal. Just wow. That's it.

Ratchet the vernacular like the dickens [133]

this Mayor of East Village digs Reverdy too [134]

"Use blue *and name a couple friends"*

neither quite Warshed up in PoetryWorld

For Stephen—stay excited… all the way to north-

west, & back as far as Yugen (rimes w/ Dōgen)

This off-the-cuff take is on-the-button

so we'll be tender between the muttons, sign off

righty, we're gonna end with a friend

yr northern pal posts at two-gun

[133]One almost feels it's like quoting Joe Biden ("Here's the deal" & again "Here's the deal"), but this time we're quoting lines from this same JW poem in *Blue Lyre*, which I said to Jeff is "one of the best books of poetry I've read in ages."

[134]JW, the "Mayor of the East Village" (Richard Hell, quoted in *Triple Crown*).

Jan Zwicky: Zees & Zeds Tamped Down

Rot even deeper than one thinks,
gone mushy to the core; no vision, only
words. Words, words, words, words.
Mere sketches, columns, lists;

Wittgenstein Elegies — Jan Zwicky

Rot even deeper than one thinks,

a'miss or mess, slow-roll on Zees & Zeds

backup past Zasterle, Z & ZYZZYVA [135]

tamped down to maladie du pulp (oh, again)

gone mushy to the core; no vision, only

shudder quiver shiver (slip slide tripping

round PoBiz)   Escapade's from Old Spa.

the trick, prank, gambol in cutting loose

[135]Near bygone presses & journals

words. Words, words, words, words.

Consumption every line, baby letters, commas

Zuker punch[136] tiny comas every breath

petite mort, each exhale dead on a wire

Mere sketches, columns, lists;

double-hinged -barreled / bi- tri-columnar

Shall we dance these around again

last gloss on — say ray hey — you?

[136]Mark Zukerberg (FB's disingenuous, smirky face) refers to himself as an "ona'peneur"—can't argue with that, these plastic neoliberal times. (Happi'ne'ess is a warm gun," as John Lennon put it.) Yo!

Jennifer Bartlett: I Sing to You

When I write I think about Lisa Jarnot. When I write I think about Andrea.

. . .

When I write, I think about Duncan and Eigner and Bob. When I think about Bob

When I Write — Jennifer Bartlett *(with little nods to bp & The Hollies, & F. Mac)*

When I write I think about Lisa Jarnot. When I write I

can see where this is going — 2338 McGee Avenue [137]

let's jump on it, ahead of those praiseworthy saints, rascals

misheard in the rain, bare-assing under my um'bre'lla

think about … [*tomorrow*]

think about a long St Roll on a short St Reet

tappin' it out in good time …   these are my

words / what history teaches / I sing to you

---

[137]Communal house in Berkeley shared by poet friends Robert (Bob) Grenier, Kathleen Frumkin, & Larry Eigner (the subject of Jennifer Bartlett's upcoming biography).

When I write, I think about Duncan and Eigner

about CanPoets for GoFundMe — her bio knows

Dis/ability's [138] no joke, don't trip up this deft & dy-

namite poet, no Black Barts sunk in Po-Wars [139]

and Bob. When I think about Bob

eye's thinking uncles & every bob in the barrel

tapinosis (a'gyne eh) [140] all the way from two-gun

to two-pun danced thru the tunes of PoWorld

---

[138]See powerful essays on "Dis/ability" (& on poetry's corrupt Prize Culture), in Shane Neilson's *Constructive Negativity.*

[139]Black Bart Poetry Society, & the hilarious '80s Bay Area "Poetry Wars" (Black Mtn vs LangPo— fathers & sons, inc.)

[140]USAmericans in boarding school razed us local Canucks: "a'gyne & a'gyne & a'gyne, eh, duh-boys?"

derek beaulieu: a 'pataphysics of imaginary solutions

Poetry is the last refuge of the unimaginative.
Poetry has little to offer outside of poetry itself. Poets chose to be poets because they do not have the drive to become something better. / *Please, no more poetry.*

Please, No More Poetry — derek beaulieu *(with nods to glosa'd Dworkin, Jones, Thesen, & Bernstein)*

Poetry is the last refuge of the unimaginative.

Novel deaths rotate in public / dime a dozen / on the axis

poetry should mine big gaps with art's hearsay praxis [141]

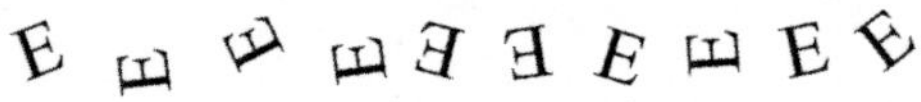

Poetry has little to offer outside of poetry itself. Poets chose to

sit on the shelf, [142] spite their fece, pat their physic

bash heads with imaginary solutions, un-ripple every pond

dis guy can boilerplate Concrete to VisPo, ConceptPo, & beyond

---

[141]The three derek beaulieu concrete lines that follow are from *Kern* (p.87) & *Xerolage* (p.3)

[142]Peter Ackroyd, in one of his novels, makes passing reference to an annual 500 unread books of poetry collecting dust on the National Library's shelves. (♪ 500 miles, 500 miles ♪…)

be poets because they do not have the drive to become something

veered south, one arm steer-wheelers road testing the LangPo

yr duty (an era / any time / of year [143]) maintain plant, westward haut

g g g g g g g

better. / *Please, no more poetry.*

flat on its back… B B B B B B

Raw is an aversion to the conservative dogmas of worry.

Rrose Sélavy is never having to say you're sorry.

[143]Fiddling with Zukofsky, of course: "*A*"-22

Guy Birchard: A Perfect Disdain

Live the consequences as if each day be second-
last. From Paradise ejected, perdition abide.
No hay remedio. *Honour what is holy.* Viva la
causa. *An entire life is only one allegory.*

Only Seemly — Guy Birchard *(with multi-nods to Guy Birchard, & a noodle to the other GB)*

Live the consequences as if each day be second-

or one, everywhere of nowhere, GB of garret bedsit

not Kerri's dale Under da radar guy, disaffiliated

Lay poet By the blood… what are the odds

last. From Paradise ejected, perdition abide.

Where drill down (deep dive) into yr narrative, eh?

Irreducible, credulous, diffident, misprized

Master of all — unglossed, uncraven, unalloyed [144]

---

[144]Mina & Arthur again, unboxed (hoho); see "MR" glosa

No hay remedio. *Honour what is holy.* Viva la
la'la avant-kitsch, embedded by rodomontade
not about but bound to end SOL & SFA, of
No Fixed Address — preserved from celebrity

causa. *An entire life is only one allegory.*
A clark's throw on the O-line, re-route to a
Small Provincial Capital of Dreadful Night (home
Lord / knows / He owes / us *no / reward* [145]

[145]A big footnote on the inestimably brilliant GB, in his *own* words: Guy Birchard began, lives presently, and appears not about but bound to end in Canada. // Scholar of nothing. No degrees. No prizes. Neither profession, trade nor career. // "Ineducable, / credulous, diffident, laconic, single-minded, / misprized" // A poet preserved from celebrity, admiring craft, aspiring to art. // A lay poet. // "a man of no rank come to a place without merit." // … sells books and booze at Moose Jaw, Sask. // [whose books] May they outlive me. What are the odds. // I am *enfin* an aging poet of whom most likely you will not have heard. No oversight of your own. I passed time in several capitals and their lands… incognito by birth. // "Senior's Home Address: Small Provincial Capital of Dreadful Night." (From poems, Forewords, End Pages, & Back Covers: *Further than the Blood*; *Only Seemly*; *Hecatomb*; *Twenty Grand*; *Aggregate Retrospective*; this poet is surely, of all, the most real deal.)

Nick Demske: Eponymous Debut

... I will make me beautiful if it takes
Uglying everything else... I will beat these
Precious children back to life. Fuck me, shit me.
Remind me what it's like to be offended, Nick Demske.

Common Sense — Nick Demske (*with a couple extra nods to Nick Demske*)

... I will make me beautiful if it takes

a postcard on my desk to KEEP POETRY UGLY [146]

obliterate all targets, such *offhand finesse*

yr *eponymous debut* — my new pony [147]

Uglying everything else... I will beat these

ducklings silly, beat me (twice), a Gregorian calendar

Nick Demske is the poet laureate of your face [148]

all dat jazzy sassy punchy — simile'd on da reader's face

---

[146]A favourite postcard from Ugly Duckling Presse
[147]Some phrasing here from Jeff Wright's review of Nick Demske's *Nick Demske*, Brooklyn Rail (Dec'10-Jan '11 Issue)
[148] Line from Nick Demske's website

Precious children back to life. Fuck me, shit me.

Nod me Dave Chappelle's taking the piss, 20% alphabet

letters they Love to Grate each other Bad Too Quick

Tell us what to feel & say / Reward us with a grant today [149]

Remind me what it's like to be offended, Nick Demske.

enjamb that promise up the Muse's tuchis, Oulipo to Newlipo

If i ERASE my face it opens another ERA any time of year

Point and click. Smile. You've just been [ah] *Nick Demsked.*

[149]Paraphrased lines in Rachel Blau DuPlessis' *Late Work*, p. 100

Elaine Equi: Talk Us Thru Your Devices

I don't want to have to use a multiplatform verification system
that requires three different devices to open a piece of spam.
We need better places to hide our innate incendiary worthlessness.
Like poems, for example. Nobody would think to look there.

We Don't Need Another Psychic — Elaine Equi *(with nods, & a bonus half-line)*

I don't want to have to use a multiplatform verification system

drill down in weeds dese flarfed up cancel culture narrative

erase dis existential mare, trailer park conspiracy's walk-us-thru

Lower limit noise [150] (who needs poise?) find these boys wld be bhoys

that requires three different devices to open a piece of spam.

Green eggs & ham, click here — Martian radio, white & aimless

signals, repurpos'd lightbulb flick a flimflam on the web-scam

Have adenoidal twang, will slam & scram (this lame o'sham

[150]Equi's fine take in "Zukofsky Revision," *Sentences and Rain*, p. 74

We need better places to hide our innate incendiary worthlessness.
Crawl inside der cyberpunk road-tester, drive yr keyboard wire-
less is more anarcho 'n agitprop, dig into Bardy Google guy
serial decoder on the fly, down das rabbit hole need not apply

Like poems, for example. Nobody would think to look there.
No one listens… keep Po uglier on the road, real outsider
testing one, two, three yo! unpack lost bunnies they're on show
poètes maudits extraordinaire — Elaine Equi: meet Edward Dorn
(no one else wld dare to scorn

Phil Hall: Country's Finest Living Daylights

soon they'll be kicking the daylights out of some asshole
who looks like Phil Hall the poet
these living *daylights*
I sing

Bottom — Phil Hall *(with nods to further Halls)*

soon they'll be kicking the daylights out of some asshole

doesn't stand up for free or thee *Canadian Shield White Trash*

(talks real Can-eh-jun, eh, prob'ly from pray'ries

maybe Win'sor, Ont-A-A-rio

who looks like Phil Hall the poet

says "Zukofsky couldn't type drive or sing… [&]

Music doesn't care wasn't there

at the end won't pretend it was" [151]

[151]These three lines from Hall's "Cadence" (*The Small Nouns Crying Faith*)

these living *daylights*

asshole'd or no, one of

the country's finest

living lights

I sing

— undressed mouth [152] —

word it   name it

it doesn't drag [153]

[152]Hall, "Undressed" (*Niagara & Government*): "I undressed my mouth"
[153]Stan Dragland, *The Difficult*: "Phil Hall fled a bleak Ontario upbringing among what he has called 'Canadian Shield White Trash'. He was escaping 'Silence—ignorance—bitterness—crudity—xenophobia—contempt for all that is fanciful (books *etc*)—addiction—violence—misogyny'.... he carries all that early stuff still... though it was many books before he began to acknowledge, word it, name it." (*The Difficult*, p. 67)

Kent Johnson: How to Write an Avant-Garde Poem

All you have to do is look around you
at other poets… and see what unkind, impolite,
and self-involved people they are, the poets, mainly out
for themselves and their 'poetry careers', and the bigger / their vitas…

Poetry Will Save Your Life — Kent Johnson *(with gracias nods to da notes at the foot)*

All you have to do is look around you

"You like the writers in my class / The way they kiss each other's ass" [154]

breathe lilty frilly breeze thru PoEms a'loud in camp

so sigh, my PoVoice did this to me & my vo'cabs [155]

at other poets… and see what unkind, impolite

killer kitsch they loves to huh-8, dis hologram hoaxter

dis provocateur, plagiarist, poetomachia dispatch forger [156]

infamy clang his name egg-shell walking PoWorld

---

[154]From KJ's poem "The Discs of Snow" (*Big House*); & much phrasing throughout here owing to illuminating articles on KJ's *Big House*, by Sharon Thesen, Miriam Nichols, Joshua Weiner, Adam Lehrer, Paul Nelson, & Burt Kimmelman

[155]The odiously fluffed up & all too familiar "Poetry Voice" at public readings; &, with respect, repurposing Spicer's final line

[156]Johnson & Boughn's *Dispatches from the Poetry Wars*; & KJ's "Emily Post-Avant"

and self-involved people they are, the poets, mainly out

'n abt revolving doors' PoFound... float cash BigPharmaDough

dems preening petty peevish, dems hipper-than-thou

co-opt good as beat down our gone-done hippie-domes

for themselves and their 'poetry careers', and the bigger / their...

All Because of Poetry I Have a Big House on the Oceans (Both), 3

fuckin Cars, Piles of MooLa, and Really mucho much sex! [157] My third

ex-wife once asked me, "How to Write an Avant-Garde Poem. No shit." [158]

---

[157]The most excellent full title of the present KJ book of poems
[158]First part of line, from this present, glossed KJ poem; the quote is from Joshua Weiner's "Antidisestablishmentarianism: A Too Personal Thunk on Kent Johnson's Big House," referencing the title of a summer program course "taught by a radically chic poet...in Provincetown," circa 2000: the avant-garde co-opted & mainstreamed (yet again) to pointlessness

Duncan McNaughton: Imagine Our Surprise

(for K & M)

a poem in this day and age, it's dark, needs
to have a small flashlight and a cordless
power drill with which to remove the screws.
It needs to be a kiss / that stings.

The Kiss — Duncan McNaughton *(with nods to Saroyan glosa & all the rest, incl the kitchen sink, finito)*

a poem in this day and age, it's dark, needs

imagine our surprise…   Dylan, Sartre, social's grand

ism down to disco, its idiot grade B-worm bop-bop

bop-bop *Stayin' Alive*, well we didn't much did we

to have a small flashlight and a cordless

midnight hour of wry / arch / sardonic   right in

the guts…   uh uh uh uh stayin' alive

with the air in our heads killing us

power drill with which to remove the screws.

These strange little machines which forever mis'take

locus with focus (& rimes w/ a cheesy fromage [159]

— history, I guess with or without the comma

It needs to be a kiss / that stings.

Like the poor man says, "Poetry offers so many ways

to say Fuck You to the universe's mistakes" [160]

We were there, jaundiced & all, [161] thinking even a

clogged morning sink could put a spell on us

---

[159]Forever conflating Duncan McNaughton & David Bromige; why: archival fonds? Doubtful…

[160]From DM's poem "Utrecht," in *Somewhere in the Stream*

[161]Joe Safdie, in his review of *Somewhere* (*Dispatches*), acutely refers to DM's "jaundiced sense of humor"

Acknowledgements

Grateful acknowledgement to the editors of the following journals and special editions, where many of these poems first appeared:

Alien Buddha, Art Bar Poetry Series, Better Than Starbucks, Big Pond Rumours, BlazeVOX Journal 18, Blazing Stadium, Brave New Word, Brickyard (YouTube), The Café Review, Canadian Literature, Canadian Poetry Review, Dispatches from the Poetry Wars, Distāntia (YouTube), Empty Mirror, eratio, Event, Former People, Futures Trading, Golden Handcuffs Review, Grain Magazine, Harbinger Asylum, Interim: A Journal of Poetry & Poetics, Line Rider Press, Live Mag!, M58, Mantis, The Maynard, Moss Trill, New Mystics, Offcourse, Otoliths, Pamenar Press Magazine, Pif Magazine, Poetry Pause, Problématique, Projected Letters, Ragged Lion Press (Journal & YouTube), Streetcake, Terror House Magazine, The Typescript, X-peri.

One poem was printed in an edition of 50 copies as a folded long-sheet, by Kyle Flemmer, at The Blasted Tree Art Collective & Publishing Co.

A second poem was printed in an edition of 50 copies as a postcard, by Geoffrey Nilson, at PageFiftyOne

A third poem was printed by the League of Canadian Poets for their *Poem in Your Pocket Day* postcard booklet

Three poems will appear shortly in the Caitlin Press anthology *Hologram for PK Page*, eds, Yvonne Blomer & DC Reid.

About the Author

Stephen Bett is a widely and internationally published Canadian poet. His earlier work is known for its *sassy, edgy, hip… caustic wit—indeed, for the askance look of the serious satirist… skewering what he calls the 'vapid monoculture' of our times*. His more recent books have been called *an incredible accomplishment* for their *authentic minimalist subtlety*. Many are tightly sequenced book-length 'serial' poems, which allow for a rich echoing of cadence and image, building *a wonderfully subtle, nuanced music*. Bett follows in the avant tradition of Don Allen's *New American Poets*. Hence the mandate for Simon Fraser University's "Contemporary Literature Collection" to purchase and archive his "personal papers" for scholarly use. He is recently retired after a 31-year teaching career, largely at Langara College in Vancouver, and now lives with his wife Katie in Victoria, BC.

His website is stephenbett.com

About CHAX

Founded in 1984 in Tucson, Arizona, Chax has published more than 240 books in a variety of formats, including hand printed letterpress books and chapbooks, hybrid chapbooks, book arts editions, and trade paperback editions such as the book you are holding. From August 2014 until July 2018 Chax Press resided in Houston-Victoria Center for the Arts. Chax is a nonprofit 501(c)(3) organization which depends on suppport from various government & private funders, and, primarly, from individual donors and readers. In July 2018 Chax Press returned to Tucson. In 2021, Chax Press founder and director Charles Alexander was awarded the Lord Nose Award for lifetime achievement in literary publishing.

Our current address is 1517 North Wilmot Road no. 264, Tucson, Arizona 85712-4410. You can email us at *chaxpress@chax.org.*

Your support of our projects as a reader, and as a benefactor, is much appreciated.

You may find CHAX at *https://chax.org*

Broken Glosa has been composed in Adobe Garamond Pro

Design by Ben Lerner & Charles Alexander

Printed & Bound by KC Book Manufacturing